Z z

Bees are very busy creatures. They go from flower to flower collecting pollen and buzzing busily, *zzzzzz*.

Action: Put your arms out at your sides and flap them like a bee, saying *zzzzzz*.

buzz buzz

buzz buzz

z zz zz zz zz zz zz

zz zzz zz zz z

_ig _ag   bu_ _

est   fi _

The wind and the sun want to see who is stronger. 'I'll blow that man's coat off', says the wind – *w, w, w, w* – but the man holds on to his coat. 'My turn', says the sun, shining brightly. The man gets so hot that he takes off his coat.

W w

Action: Blow onto your open hands as if you are the wind, saying *w, w, w, w.*

west wind

west wind

W   w w w w w w

w w w w ww ww

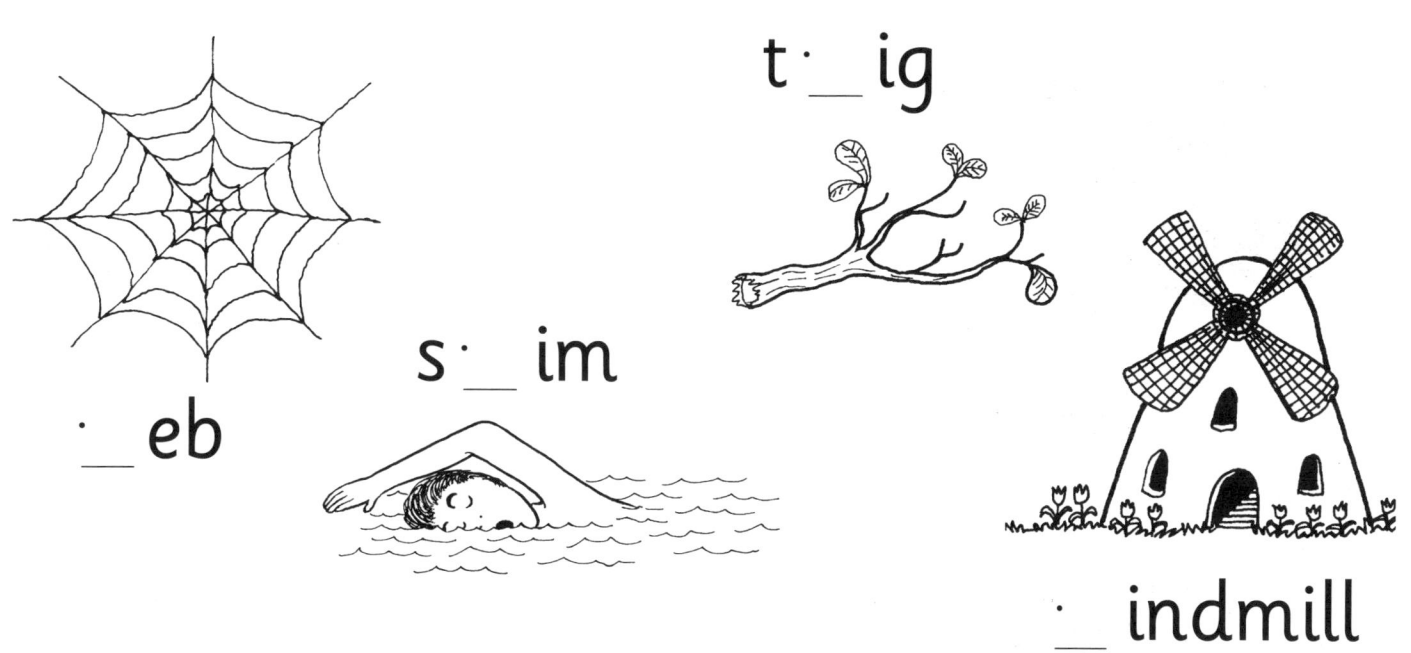

_eb   s_im   t_ig   _indmill

ng

Snake, Bee and Inky are watching a strong man lifting weights on television. They pretend to be weightlifters, too. Inky lifts a broom up over her head, saying *ng…*

Action: Pretend to be a weightlifter lifting a heavy weight above your head, and say *ng…*

strong

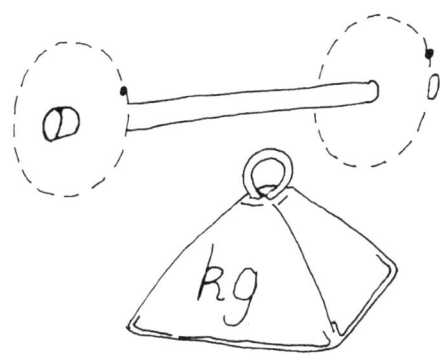
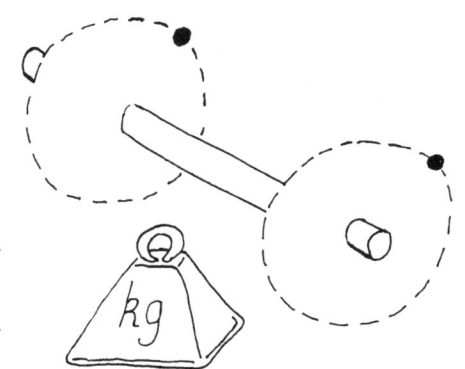

strong

ng   ng   ng   ng   ng
ng   ng   ng   ng   ng

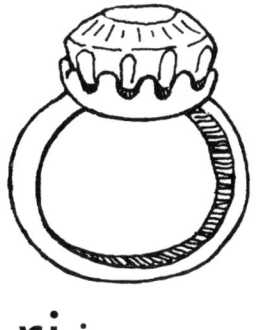
ri___

ki___

stri___

ba___

Uncle Vic is a delivery man. He is driving his van to the village to deliver some vegetables. Inky, Snake and Bee wave to Vic as he drives by, *vvvvvv*, vroom!

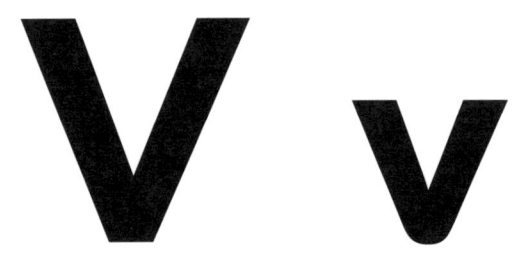

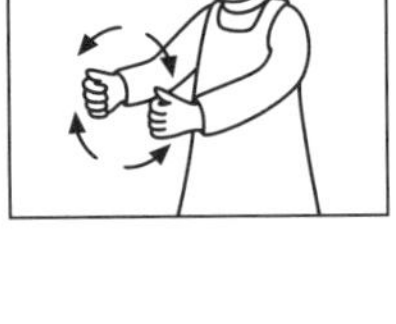

Action: Pretend to be driving along in a van, saying *vvvvvvv*.

 # Vic's van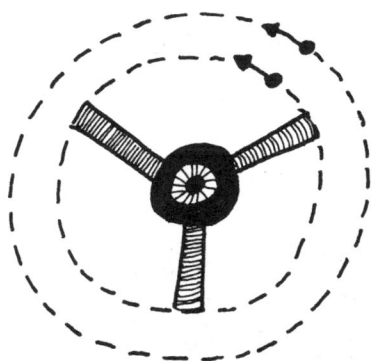

Vic's van

 v v v v v v v v v
v v v v v v v v v

_et

loa_es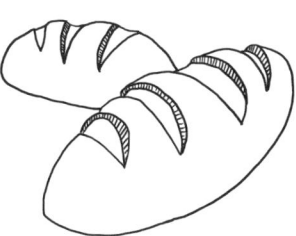

_an

se_en

To show that ‹oo› can make two different sounds, the *oo* (as in *foot*) and *oo* (as in *moon*) are shown in two different sizes.

Little oo

oo

Long oo

oo

Bee, Snake and Inky have found a cuckoo clock. The cuckoo pops in and out saying *oo, oo, oo, oo*

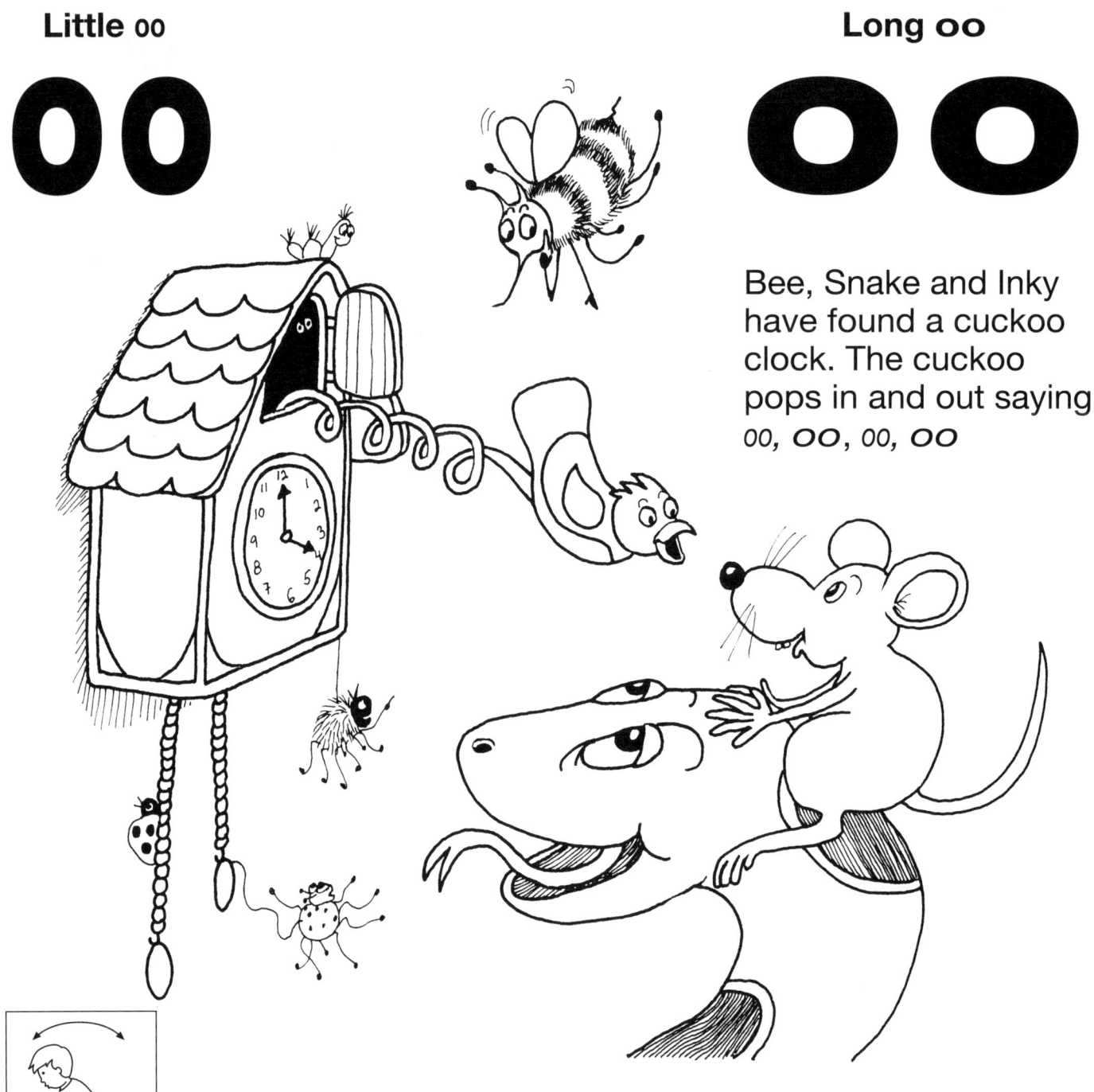

Action: Move your head back and forth like the cuckoo in a cuckoo clock, calling *oo-oo, oo-oo* (*oo* as in book, *oo* as in moon).

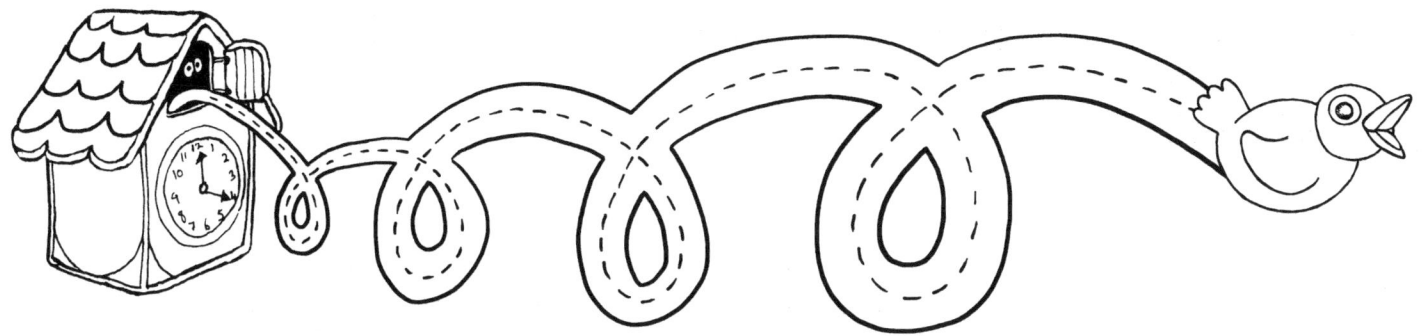

In writing, only one size of ‹oo› is used.

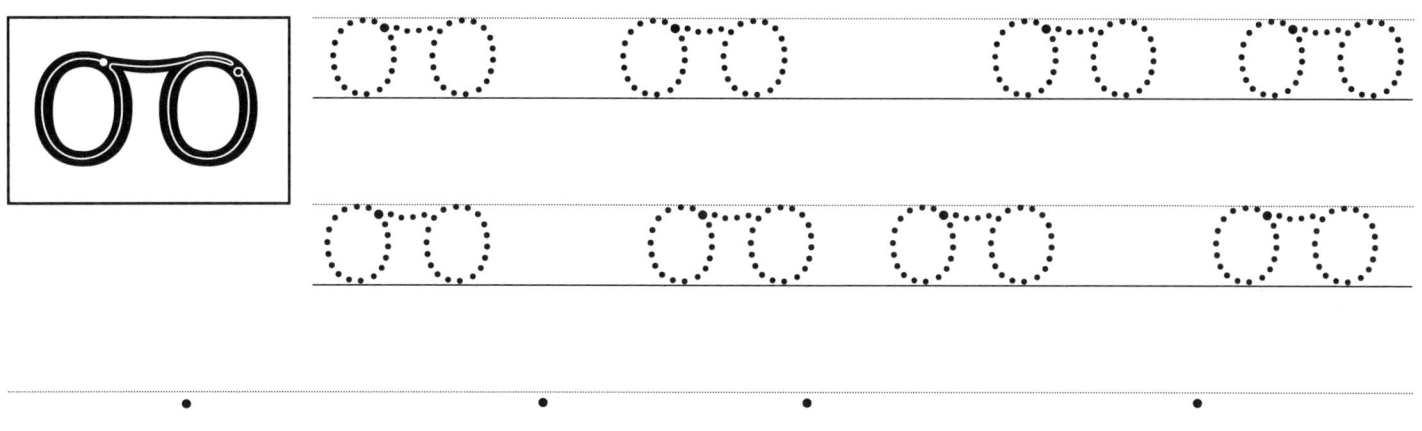

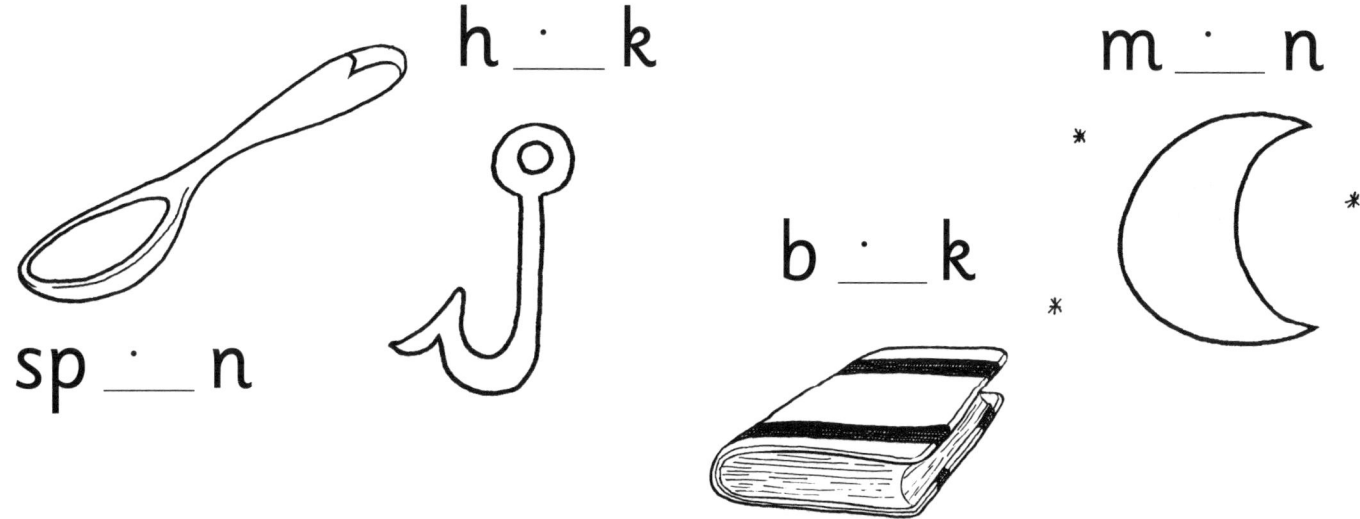

When reading, try the little /oo/ sound first. If this does not make a word, try the long /oo/ sound.

 Add ‹ng›, read the word and draw a picture.

ri<u>ng</u>   wi___   ba___

swi___   stri___   fa___s

stro___   ki___   si___

Join each word to its picture.

Join each word to its picture.

oo oo

- hook
- spoon
- broom
- foot
- moon
- boot
- wood
- book

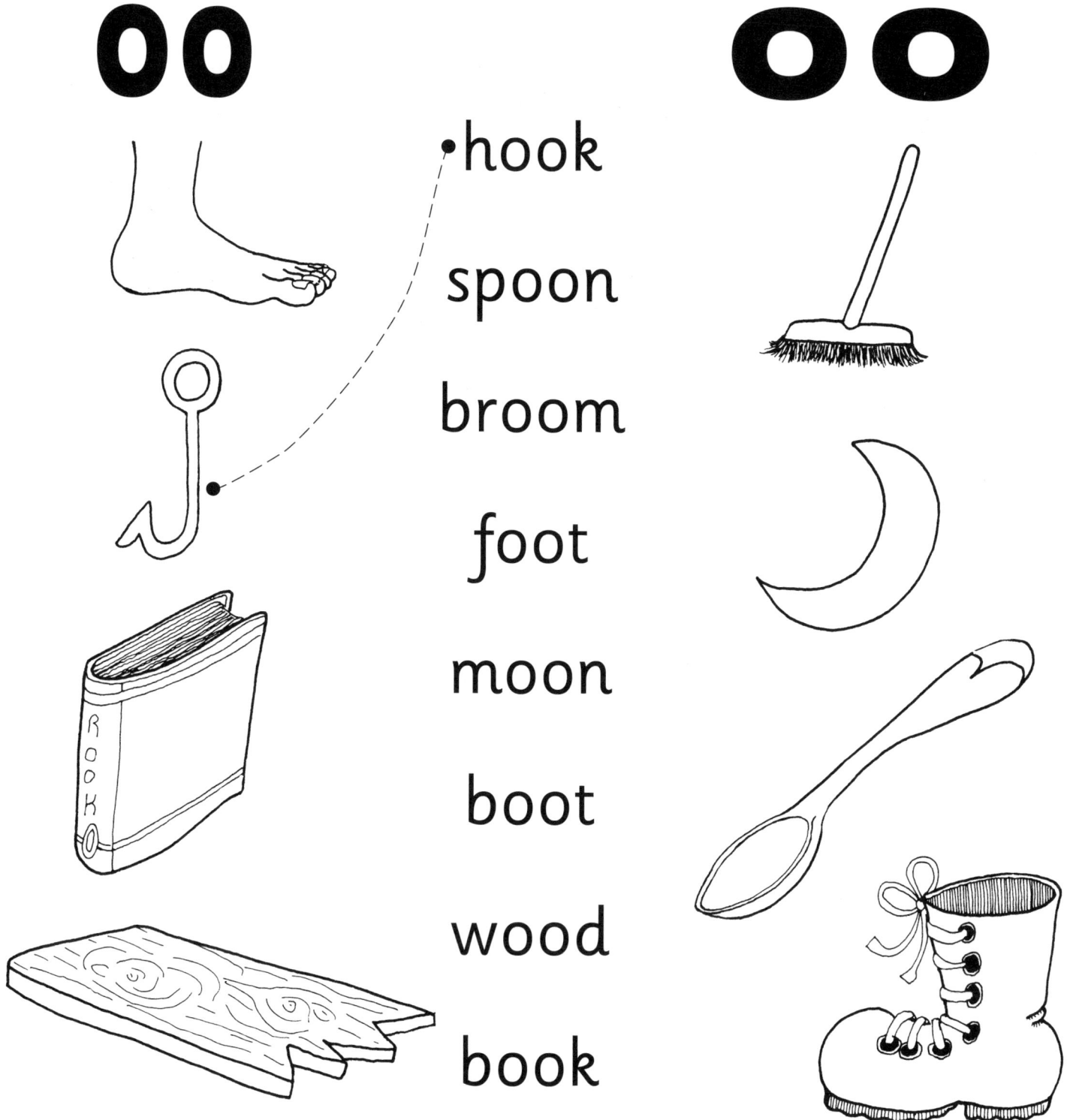

Trace over the dotted lines to help the spiders spin their webs.

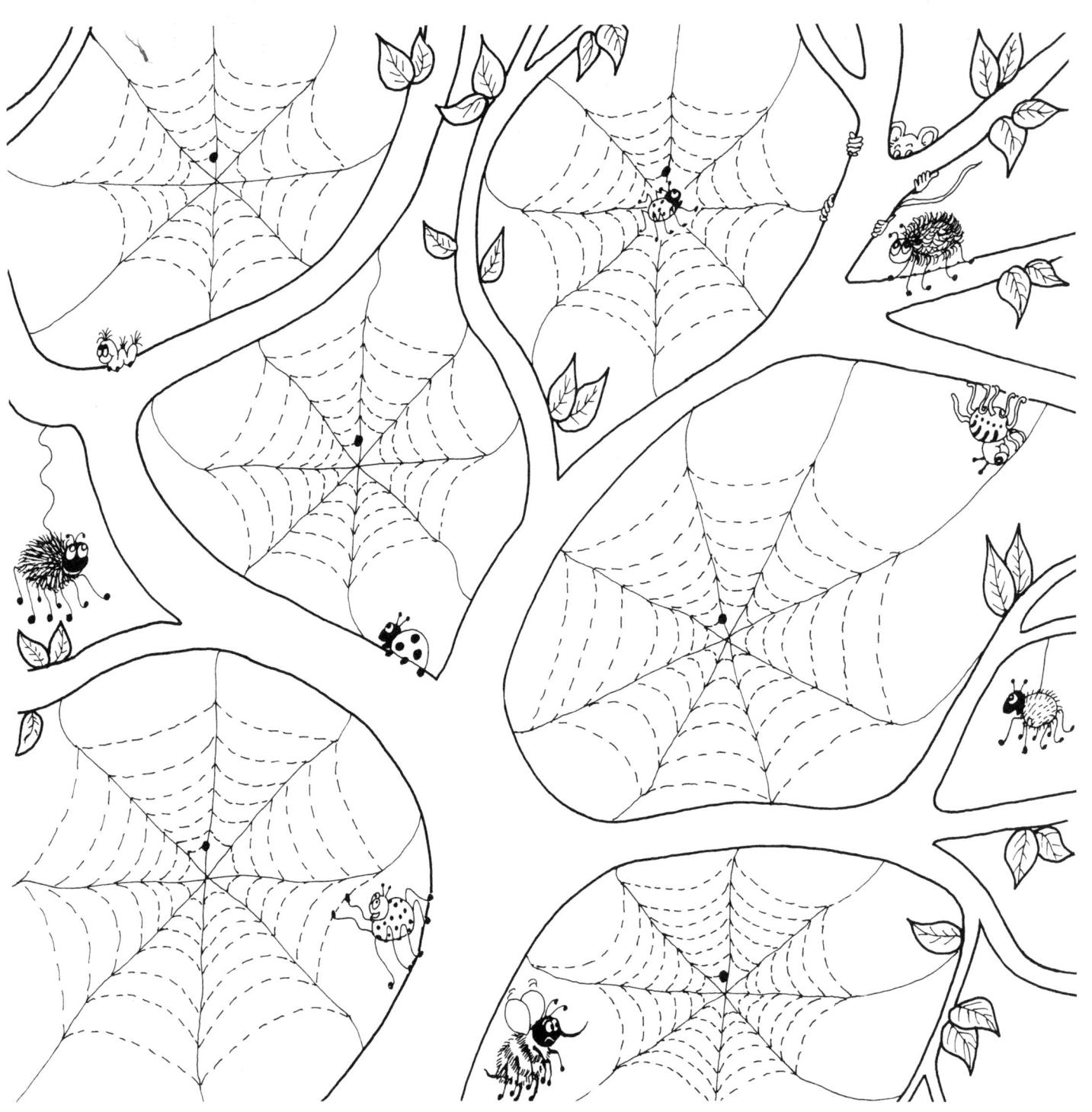

Join each phrase to its picture.

a duck on a pond

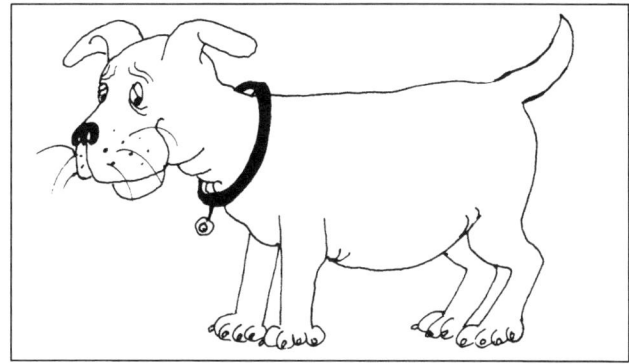

a cat and 3 kittens

a rabbit and a carrot

a big fat dog

Anagrams

Say the words, listen for the sounds and write the words.

ee t f	k f or	ng s i
oo b k	r d oa	t b oo
ai r n	l ai t	ie p

Read the words and add them to the picture.

a frog	2 ducks
a buzzing bee	the sun
a big green tree	a nest with 3 eggs

Go over the patterns, keeping on the lines. Start from the dot each time.

Say the word for each picture and listen for the sounds. Then write the letters for the sounds and read the word to check it.

21

Practise these tall letters, which have 'sticks' above the body of the letter. Note that the ‹t› is not quite as tall as the others.

1 2 3 4 5

Count the butterflies.

Trace over the dotted lines to write the number 5.

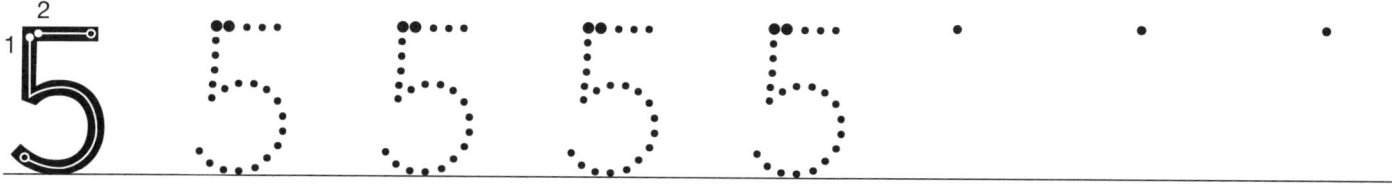

Find the 5 butterflies.

Activity

Make your own cuckoo clock

Draw your clock on a piece of card and write *oo* and *OO*. Make a cuckoo and stick it on a separate long, narrow piece of card.

Cut a slit in the doorway (indicated by white dashes in the picture) and push your cuckoo backwards and forwards, saying *oo, OO; oo, OO.*

Weightlifting

See how strong you are.

Flying bee *zzzzzzzz*

Cut out a semicircle of card. Give it yellow and black stripes and then fix the 2 sides together to form a cone. Cut some wings from tissue paper and give your bee some eyes.

Do some weighing

Can you find something that weighs less than you, or more than you?